A GREAT AQUARIUM BOOK

To Todd and Jacques

A great AQUARIUM BOOK

The putting-it-together guide for beginners

by Jane Sarnoff and Reynold Ruffins

37744

Charles Scribner's Sons, New York

Different kinds of fish live in different parts of the river. Some fish like it where the water is shallow, still, and very warm. Other fish like it where the water is deeper and cooler and where the bottom is muddy instead of sandy. All fish, of course, like it best where they can find the type of food they want and the kind of plants and rocks they need, where their neighbors are friendly and their enemies cannot follow.

Where do fish wash?

In a river basin

FROM THEIR HOME TO YOUR HOME

Freshwater tropical fish are wild animals. And working with wild animals—lions, bears, or fish—takes a lot of planning and patience.

The way to start is by treating the animal kindly and making it comfortable—giving it a home as much like its natural home as possible. Most of the fish kept in a freshwater aquarium come from the rivers of the tropics. You certainly can't give your fish a river, but with the help of *A Great Aquarium Book,* you can create a world that is very much like a small part of a tropical river.

Many different things go into building a natural river world for your fish. You must consider the kinds and numbers of fish, the space they will live in, the water, temperature, light, sunshine, fresh air, food, plants, rocks, and everyday care they will need. *A Great Aquarium Book* tells you what you need to know about these things so that you can create a basic aquarium...an aquarium that provides almost everything your fish need without a lot of fussing...an aquarium that lets you enjoy your fish and your fish enjoy life in the world you have made for them.

"Aquaria" means more than one aquarium.

*If fish lived on land
what country would they live in?*

Finland

Most fish have two names, a common name and a scientific name.
Two different fish might have the same common name in different places,
or the same fish might have two different common names,
but each fish has only one scientific name
and no other fish shares that name.

THE PARTS OF THE FISH

There are more than 30,000 kinds of fish. Each is different from the rest in some way, but there are many things about all fish that are the same. The parts of the body that are shown here are common to most fish.

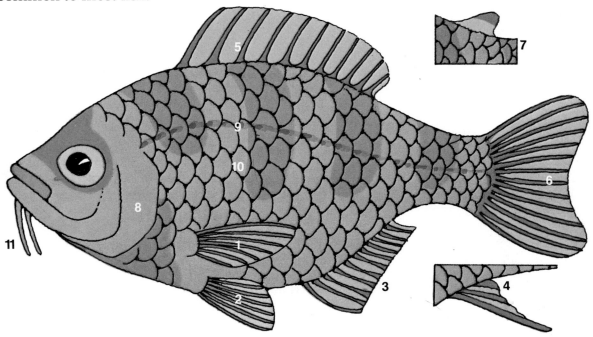

1 **Pectoral fins** *One on each side. Used for braking and steering.*

2 **Ventral or pelvic fins** *One on each side. Used in movement and steering.*

3 **Anal fin** *Helps keep fish steady. Helps stop fish from rolling over. Some male fish have a* **4 gonopodium**—*a mating organ—instead of an anal fin. It is long and pointed and looks more like a rod than a fin.*

5 **Dorsal fin** *Helps keep fish steady. Stops fish from rolling over. Changes in shape from fish to fish. May be almost any shape—short and stiff, or wide and flowing, or divided into two parts.*

6 **Caudal or tail fin** *Helps fish move forward.*

7 **Adipose fin** *An extra fin that only a few fish have.*

8 **Gill cover** *Protects the gills through which fish breathe.*

9 **Lateral line** *Allows fish to feel movement in the water. The lateral line of differently shaped scales on the outside of the fish is over a long, thin tube, filled with a thick fluid, just under the surface of the fish's skin. Special pores in the scales that make up the lateral line let the "movement" in the water touch the fluid in the tube. Then the fluid passes the message to the fish's brain. Because of the lateral line, fish don't bump into things, or each other, even if they can't see where they are going. The lateral line may look different on the outside of different fish, but the extra sense—something between feeling and hearing—is still working.*

An ichthyologist is a person who studies fish.

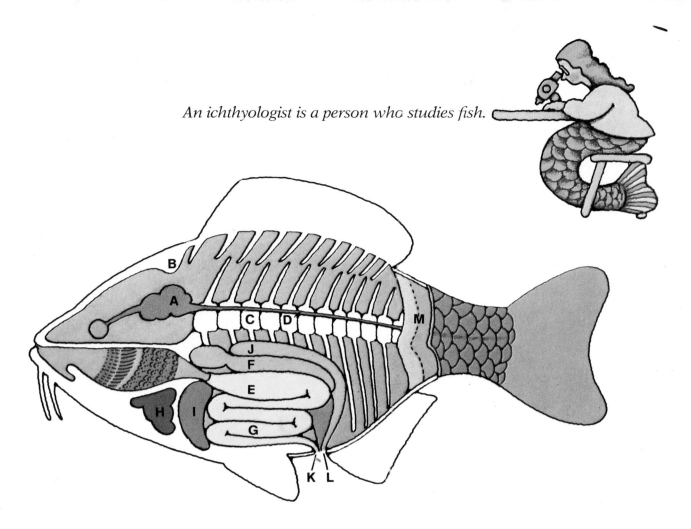

10 Scales *Overlapping scales cover most fish and protect their skin. The scales are protected by a slimy covering. The color of the fish comes from the skin under the scales. Scales themselves have no color, but they help the colors of the skin shine brightly in different directions. The color of some fish changes to match their surroundings and their feelings.*

11 Barbels *Some fish, especially those that live mostly on the bottom, have whiskers attached to the upper lip. The whiskers have taste buds that make it easier for the fish to find food even when they cannot see well.*

A   **brain**
B   **skull**
C   **spinal column**
D   **spinal nerve**
E   **stomach**
F   **air bladder**
G   **intestine**
H   **heart**
I   **liver**
J   **kidney**
K   **anus**
L   **urogenital opening**
M   **muscles**

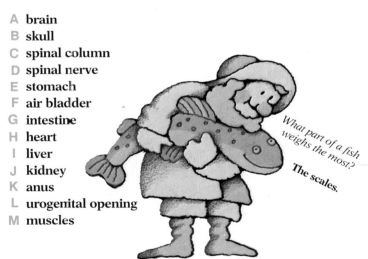

What part of a fish weighs the most?

The scales.

Which fish is most valuable? A goldfish

More than one fish in water or a museum can be called either *fish* or *fishes*.
More than one fish in a frying pan are always called *fish*.

The young of fish are, in general, called fingerlings or fry. The young of some fish, however, have special names. Young eels are elvers; young codfish are codlings or sprang. Young sharks are called cubs; young salmon are parr, smolt, or grilse. Young mackerel are called spike, blinker, or tinker.

A group of fish is usually called a school, but it can also be called a draught. A group of whales (which are not fish but sea mammals) can be called a gam or a pod.

Fish can be spelled **ghoti:**
The **gh** as in *enough;*
the **o** as in *women;*
the **ti** as in *nation.*

The Greeks used to believe that everything on land could also be found underwater. The names of some fish make that seem true. There are catfish and dogfish, frogfish and toadfish, lionfish and tigerfish, cowfish, pigfish, and rabbitfish. There are batfish, scorpionfish, snakefish, and butterfly fish, turkeyfish and parrotfish, wolf fish, and even a sea robin and a sea horse.

Five frail fish fled from fear for four feeding fish flashed forth.
(Say that five times fast.)

WHICH FISH?

Choosing the fish to put into an aquarium is always very difficult. There are so many that are just too interesting and exciting not to have. Only a few fish are pictured and discussed here, but they have been carefully chosen for special reasons...

All the fish can live under the same conditions. A community tank—a tank with many different kinds of fish—needs fish that can live in the same type of world, sharing the space and getting along together. The fish shown here can be put together to create an almost endless number of different community tanks. Goldfish are not included, since they need different conditions—colder water, different food, more cleaning.

All the fish are "easy" fish. They don't get sick often, they aren't too fussy about food and other living conditions, and, if you make a few mistakes, they can usually still survive.

Almost all of the different kinds of habits and behavior that you can find in tropical fish can be found in these fish. Fish with habits or needs that make them particularly hard to raise have been left out.

All of the fish are available in most pet stores.

Some of the fish swim mostly at the top of the tank, others mostly near the middle or the bottom. Still others swim everywhere. Each tank should have some fish at each level. That way each type of fish has more swimming room and the tank is more interesting to watch.

Look for fish to buy that are active and alert-looking. Check to see that they are doing what they are supposed to be doing—swimming back and forth, eating algae, hiding in plants. If a fish is swimming oddly, has sagging fins, or is in a tank that has dead fish in it—forget it.

The fish discussed in this book give birth one of three ways. They bear live young, lay eggs, or build bubble nests. The information given about the fish tells which does which, but does not include breeding instructions. It's best to set up and maintain a few good community tanks first, before you start thinking about breeding fish. Of course, some fish, particularly live-bearers such as guppies, may think about breeding before you do. Talk to the pet store people fast!

all level fish

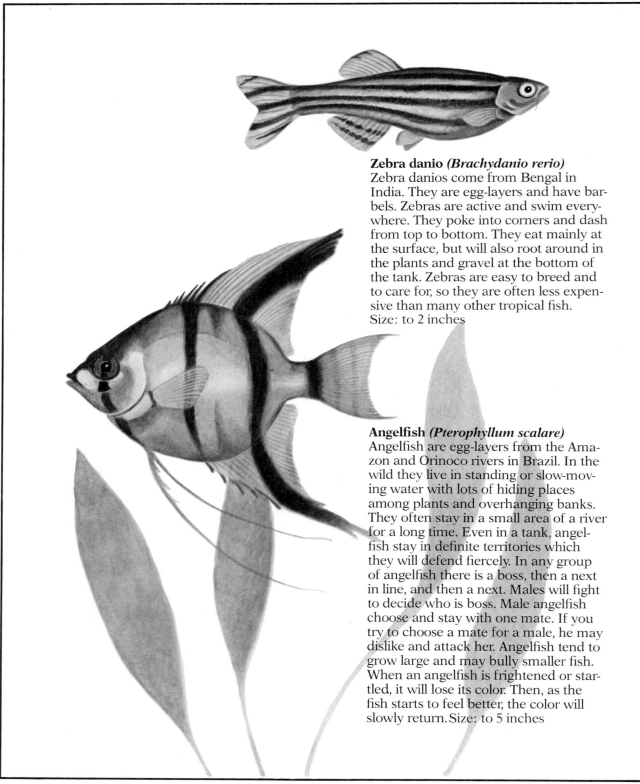

Zebra danio *(Brachydanio rerio)*
Zebra danios come from Bengal in India. They are egg-layers and have barbels. Zebras are active and swim everywhere. They poke into corners and dash from top to bottom. They eat mainly at the surface, but will also root around in the plants and gravel at the bottom of the tank. Zebras are easy to breed and to care for, so they are often less expensive than many other tropical fish.
Size: to 2 inches

Angelfish *(Pterophyllum scalare)*
Angelfish are egg-layers from the Amazon and Orinoco rivers in Brazil. In the wild they live in standing or slow-moving water with lots of hiding places among plants and overhanging banks. They often stay in a small area of a river for a long time. Even in a tank, angelfish stay in definite territories which they will defend fiercely. In any group of angelfish there is a boss, then a next in line, and then a next. Males will fight to decide who is boss. Male angelfish choose and stay with one mate. If you try to choose a mate for a male, he may dislike and attack her. Angelfish tend to grow large and may bully smaller fish. When an angelfish is frightened or startled, it will lose its color. Then, as the fish starts to feel better, the color will slowly return. Size: to 5 inches

Two inches = five centimeters

1
2 inches
5 centimeters

Hatchetfish *(Gasteropelecus levis)*
Hatchetfish are egg-layers, but they seldom breed in captivity. They are found mostly in northern South America. Male and female hatchetfish look much the same in size and color. They may be marbled or striped, and both male and female grow to be about 2 inches long. They are peaceful but active, and like to swim around the plants at the top of the tank. Hatchetfish spend most of their time at the surface of the tank. In fact, they are really flying fish. They can easily leap out of the water and fly long distances with their pectoral fins beating strongly. The tank must be kept covered, but plenty of breathing space should be left between the glass cover and the water surface.

Pearl danio *(Brachydanio albolineatus)*
Pearl danios are egg-layers from Burma. Although they are very active and flash around the tank, they spend most of their time at the surface level. Don't keep pearl danios in a crowded tank—they move around a lot looking for food, friends, and fun. Pearl danios grow to be about 2½ inches long. They are very hard to net because they move so fast—be careful not to hurt them. Danios have little hairlike barbels growing from the upper lip.

middle level fish

Cherry Barb *(Capoeta titteya)*
Cherry barbs are egg-layers from India. They are very active fish and do not like to be crowded. Don't put them in a community tank with too many other middle level fish. Both the male and the female are red and grow to about 2 inches in length. The male turns a brighter red when mating.

Rosy Barb *(Puntius conchonius)*
The rosy barb looks much like the cherry barb, but it has black fins and some green on its back. The female, like most female tropical fish, is not as bright in color as the male. Rosy barbs are very active, healthy, and hardy. When they are full-grown, about 2½ to 3 inches, they sometimes become bullies. If you get a really nasty one that is hurting smaller fish, take it out of the tank. Barbs belong to the same family as goldfish—the carp family.

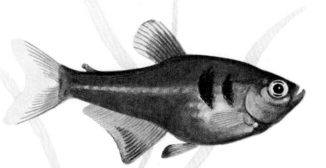

Flame or Red Tetra
(Hyphessobryco flammeas)
Flame tetras are egg-layers found in both South America and South Africa. Although they are good-looking fish, they are less bright than their name suggests. They have an adipose fin. Flame tetras are small—about 1¼ inches—and are healthy, easygoing, and undemanding. They live to be about three or four years old, which is quite a long time for such a small fish.

Cardinal Tetra
(Cheirodon axelrodi)

Cardinal tetras, like their relatives the flame tetras, come from South America and South Africa. They are more colorful than the flame tetras, but otherwise look much the same, including an adipose fin. Cardinals are easy to keep in a community tank, and enjoy swimming in small schools. They may be more expensive than the flame tetras because they are difficult to breed in great numbers.   Size: to 2 inches

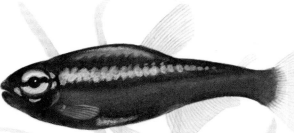

Platy or Moonfish
(Xiphophorus maculatus)

Platies are live-bearers from Southern Mexico and Guatemala. They are many-colored, and no two look exactly alike. Platies are active but good-natured, and they get along well in a community tank. The females are larger than the males, as is often true with tropical fish. The females are about 2 inches long, the males only about 1½ inches. The males have a gonopodium instead of an anal fin. Platies need algae—tiny green plants—to eat, so be sure the tank isn't too well scraped.

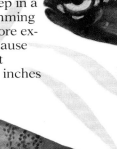

Kissing Gourami
(Helostoma temmincki)

Kissing gourami are found in Thailand, Java, Borneo, Sumatra, and the Malay Peninsula. They *should* breed by building bubble nests, like the rest of their family, but instead they float their eggs on the surface of the water. Although kissing gourami can grow to be about 4 inches long, most of them never get bigger than 2 inches. They have thick lips that stick out over tiny teeth, and can easily eat algae off of rocks and plants. Kissing gourami only look like they are kissing. No one really knows what they are doing when they touch lips, except that it is not part of mating.

Don't think that there is anything wrong if you see your kissing gourami at the surface of the tank gulping air. Gourami are labyrinth fish: they have a special body structure near the gills that lets them breathe air directly from the atmosphere as well as from the water.

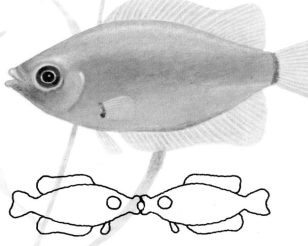

They are usually good-natured, but they may chase other fish. Kissing gouramis live two to three years in captivity.

bottom fish

Bronze Catfish (*Corydoras aeneus*)
Bronze catfish come from the rivers of South America and Trinidad. They can live under all types of conditions—hot, cold, very little or very fast-moving water, even with a reduced amount of oxygen. They are scavengers and will eat anything, including tank wastes and algae. In the aquarium, as in its natural setting, the bronze catfish likes to hide among rocks and plants near the bottom. Instead of scales, it has a type of skin armor. It also has two pair of barbels and an adipose fin. Although the bronze catfish is an egg-layer, it seldom breeds in captivity. It grows to be 1½ to 3 inches in length. In a community tank, the bronze catfish may live up to five years.

**Siamese Algae-eater
(*Gyrinochellus aymonieri*)**
The Siamese algae-eater comes from Thailand (which used to be called Siam) and, of course, eats algae. It eats with great speed and thoroughness. If there is not much algae in your tank, give the algae-eater a bit of spinach that you have boiled in clear water. Do not use leftover dinner spinach—salt and other things that are added to it may harm the fish. The Siamese algae-eater grows to be about 3 inches long in a home tank. Although it will go wherever the algae are, it likes the bottom of the tank best. The algae-eater is fast-moving, but swims with an odd, jerky motion.

Kuhli Loach(*Acanthophthalmus kuhlii*)
The kuhli loach, which is sometimes called the snake fish, comes from Java and Sumatra, where it lives in slow-moving muddy streams. Its scientific name means "thorn eye," since it has a piece of transparent skin over its eyes for protection. It is a good scavenger and will clean out the algae and wastes from the tank. When not eating, it often hides in corners and under rocks near the bottom of the tank. It also likes to curl around plant stems. In the dark, or when it becomes used to the light, it becomes more active. The kuhli loach has been known to grow to about 4 inches long, but most stop growing at about 2½ inches. The loach is a bubble nest builder, but it does not often breed in captivity.

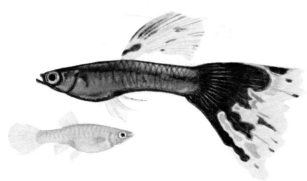

Guppy *(Lebistes reticulatus)*
Guppies come from Trinidad, Guyana, and Venezuela. They are often called rainbow fish because the males are many different colors—and no two are alike. The males grow to about 1 inch in length. The females, which are silver gray, grow to about 1½ to 2 inches.

Guppies usually stay in the upper or middle levels of the tank. They are not at all shy and often show off.

They are live-bearers and the female has from six to sixty young at a time. The adults sometimes eat the young, so there should be some floating plants for them to hide in.

Guppies can live nicely in a community tank, but they do better with their own kind. Also, because they breed so easily, it is fun to start them in their own tank. Guppies need less space than most tropical fish, but be careful about overcrowding. They will live up to three years in an aquarium.

Siamese Fighting Fish *(Betta splendens)*
Bettas are bubble nest builders from Thailand and Malaya. They grow to be about 2½ to 3 inches long. The male has flowing fins and is brightly colored. The female has smaller fins and is duller in color. Bettas are usually either mainly cornflower blue or bright red, but there are many variations. No matter what color bettas are, they are almost always extraordinarily beautiful.

Males will fight with other males and sometimes with females. In their native Thailand, male bettas are raised for sport and are put together to fight. When there is only one male in a tank, he seems lazy and peaceful. But, if you hold a mirror next to the tank, he will think that there is another male betta in the tank and will take the fighting stance.

One male betta can be kept in a bowl or a 1-gallon aquarium. The water should be kept warm and changed every week. If possible, the tank should have a plant or two. A single male or a male and a few females can also do well in a community tank. If the male attacks a female, however, the female should be removed. If it doesn't get hurt fighting, a betta will live to be about a year and a half old.

not for a first tank

Swordtail *(Xiphophorus helleri)*
Swordtails are beautiful—bright red and black. But they tend to be nasty, chase all the other fish, and hog all the food. Since they get quite large (up to 5 inches), they quickly become a problem. You could try one after the aquarium has been settled for a year or so and the other fish are used to each other. If the swordtail causes trouble, however, take it out of the tank.

Mollie *(Mollienesia latipinna)*
Mollies—especially black mollies—are nice-looking fish with a huge dorsal fin that looks like a sail. But they really need different water, higher temperatures, and more algae than is reasonable for a community tank. Some do manage to live in the usual community tank, but too often they sicken and die.

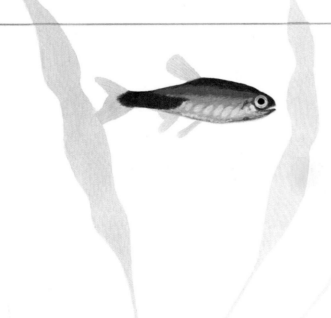

Neon Tetra *(Hyphessobrycon innesi)*
Neons are very popular, and many people will suggest that you start with a few. Unfortunately, neons often get a disease for which there is no cure. It appears as a whitish patch on the body beneath the dorsal fin. All too quickly the disease will spread to all the other fish in the tank. If you get a neon and notice such a patch, get rid of the sick fish at once and watch the other fish carefully.

EVERYTHING BUT THE FISH...

To keep your fish comfortable and healthy, and to make your aquarium easy to take care of, there are seven important things to consider:

Space·Air·Temperature·Light·Furnishings·Food·Housekeeping

When these seven things, and the fish, are all working together, you have a tank that is called "balanced." When one or more of these things gets out of order, the tank is unbalanced...and you need to do some work.

SPACE

Fish need plenty of water and space to move around in. They need room for exercise and for play. More important, they need breathing room. Fish breathe the oxygen in the water, and too many fish in too small a space use up the oxygen too fast. When you choose the size and shape of your tank, you are really deciding how many fish you can have without crowding them into too small a space with too little oxygen.

the size of the tank

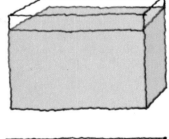

One gallon A 1-gallon tank, or even a large jar, is big enough for a single betta. The betta doesn't need any other equipment. It would like a plant or two, but they aren't necessary. Do be sure, however, to change the water, keep the tank clean, and not to overfeed.

Five gallon A pair of guppies, or even a small school of four to six guppies, can live in a 5-gallon tank if you use a small air pump, a filter, and a heater. (All equipment is discussed later in the book.) The tank should also have some floating plants for newborn guppies to hide in. Because guppies breed so easily, you will have to remove most of the young or your tank will quickly become overcrowded.

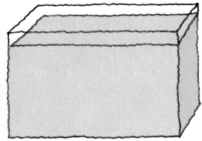

Ten and fifteen gallon About ten to twenty fish of the smaller size (1 to 1½ inches) can be kept in these aquaria without over-crowding. An air pump, a filter, and a heater will help to keep the tank clean and healthy. Although the 15-gallon size is often used for a community tank, you may outgrow it quickly or be tempted to overcrowd it.

Twenty gallon A 20-gallon tank may sound BIG...but it is really the best size for a first community tank. It gives you, and your fish, room to grow. It is, in fact, big enough for almost any variety of tropical fish. A 20-gallon tank is easier to take care of because mistakes only lead to minor problems instead of the emergencies that might occur in a smaller tank. An air pump, heater, and filter can be used to keep the tank in good condition, but you still must be careful not to overcrowd.

One gallon = 3.8 liters
Twenty gallons = 76 liters

Why do goldfish always seem so well traveled?
Because they have been around the globe.

the shape of the tank

Air enters water through the surface—the top of the tank. It is the amount of surface area, not the amount of water, that decides how much oxygen is in the water. Tall, narrow tanks and fancy-shaped tanks don't let much air into the water. An old-fashioned, fat-bellied goldfish bowl, filled to its widest part, will let in more air than the same bowl filled to the very top.

Fancy-shaped tanks are also sometimes the wrong shape to let fish swim comfortably. They can't swim up and down all the time! If you already have an oddly shaped tank, fill it to its widest point, keep very few fish in it...and save your money for a regular rectangular tank.

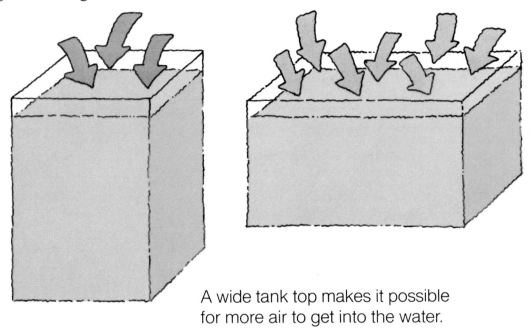

A wide tank top makes it possible for more air to get into the water.

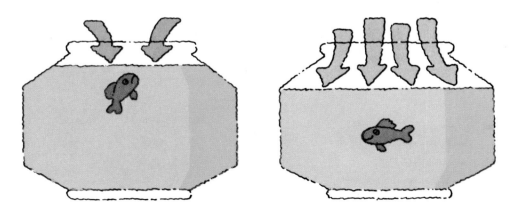

Buy a tank made of glass rather than plastic—plastic scratches easily.

AIR

In order to breathe, fish need clean water with plenty of air (oxygen) in it. In nature there are many things at work that keep the water clean and full of air. Plants help clean the water. The wind adds air to the water when it blows across the surface. Small streams feed into larger bodies of water, adding air and carrying away wastes.

You can, and should, put plants in your tank. You can also give your tank artificial wind—with an air pump—and an artificial stream—with a filter. Your fish, however, should not have to depend on artificial things to live. Pumps and filter can break down. The biggest help in keeping a tank clean and airy is not overcrowding, overfeeding, or overheating.

Some people—even people who run fish stores and know a lot about fish—will tell you that having an air pump and filter means that you can add lots of extra fish. Not so. You can add *some* extra fish, but not too many. An air pump can add air, and a filter can clean away the extra wastes, but neither can add extra living and swimming space to the tank.

If you want to see the air in water, fill a glass halfway with cold water and put it in the sun. In a few hours the sides of the glass will be covered with tiny bubbles of air.

Fish are really breathing when they look as if they are swallowing water. The water goes into the fish's mouth and out through the gills on either side of the head. The gills, just under the gill covers, remove the oxygen (air) from the water.

20

air pump

An air pump is a small electric motor that does two things: it aerates (puts air into) the water, and it runs the filter.

To get air into the water, the pump is attached to one end of a tube. On the other end of the tube, which is in the water, is a stone with tiny holes in it. The stone is called an air stone. The air pump moves air through the tube and forces it into the air stone, and the air stone lets the air into the water as tiny bubbles. Some of the air bubbles break in the water; others rise to the surface and break. The bubbles that break open on the surface act the way wind does in nature. They ruffle the surface of the water and make it easier for oxygen to get into the water and carbon dioxide to get out.

A 20-gallon community tank, and all smaller tanks, can do quite well with a simple, inexpensive vibrator pump. A vibrator pump makes a humming noise when it is on, but at least you always know when the pump is working. If you get to the stage where you have three or more tanks, you can get a more expensive and noiseless piston pump.

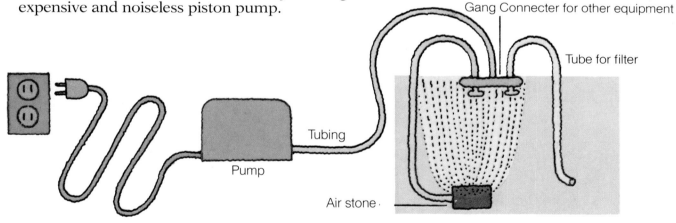

Gang Connecter for other equipment

Tube for filter

Tubing

Pump

Air stone

During the day, when it is light, plants help to aerate water by taking in the carbon dioxide that fish breathe out and giving off oxygen that the fish need to breathe in. At night, in the dark, the plants do the reverse. In a tank that has plenty of plants and is not overcrowded with fish, the air pump can be turned off during the day and turned on at night.

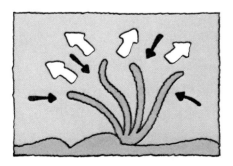

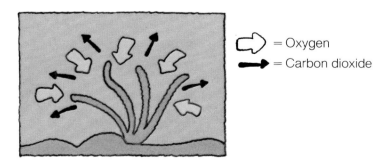

= Oxygen

= Carbon dioxide

filter

Filters are very helpful in keeping water clean, clear, and moving. Most filter units are just a container packed full of an absorbent material—often charcoal or glass wool—that traps wastes. The air pump forces water through a tube and into the filter. The wastes in the water get caught in the filter. The water stays clean, but the filter needs to be cleaned and the absorbent material changed as it gets dirty.

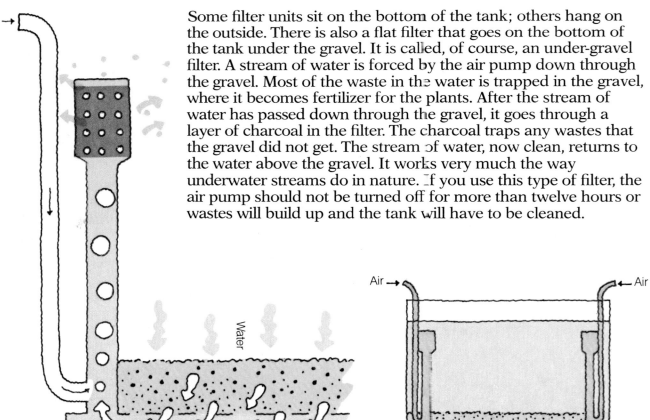

Water goes in here

Air goes in here

How a filter works

Air →

Bottom filter

Air →

Outside filter

Some filter units sit on the bottom of the tank; others hang on the outside. There is also a flat filter that goes on the bottom of the tank under the gravel. It is called, of course, an under-gravel filter. A stream of water is forced by the air pump down through the gravel. Most of the waste in the water is trapped in the gravel, where it becomes fertilizer for the plants. After the stream of water has passed down through the gravel, it goes through a layer of charcoal in the filter. The charcoal traps any wastes that the gravel did not get. The stream of water, now clean, returns to the water above the gravel. It works very much the way underwater streams do in nature. If you use this type of filter, the air pump should not be turned off for more than twelve hours or wastes will build up and the tank will have to be cleaned.

Air →

Water

How an underwater gravel filter works

Air →   ← Air

Under-gravel filter

TEMPERATURE

Fish are uncomfortable when they get too warm or too cold, and sudden and extreme changes in temperature can kill them. High temperatures take oxygen out of the water and make algae reproduce too fast. Cold water helps to spread some diseases. If you can't get the temperature exactly right, however, it is generally better to have the water a bit cooler than too warm.

heater

Most houses are not warm enough for tropical fish, and the temperature is not as constant as they need. A temperature of 72 to 78 degrees F. (22-25°C.) is about right for the fish in this book, but is rather warm for most people. The easiest way to keep your aquarium the right temperature is with an automatic aquarium heater with an attached thermostat.

You set the heater to the level you want—74 degrees F. (23°C.) will allow for changes in the house temperature and keep the water on the low side of perfect. The thermostat will turn the heater on and off automatically and keep the water at the right temperature. Different-sized heaters are needed for different-sized tanks. When you buy a heater, tell the pet store salesperson what size you have. Follow the instructions on the heater carefully and have someone check your work before you plug the heater in.

Heaters and thermostats can go wrong. So, when you buy the heater, buy an aquarium thermometer so you can be sure of the water temperature. The thermometer hangs inside the tank all the time. Make a habit of checking it regularly—and especially when there has been a big change in the weather or in the heat in your home. And remember that if the electricity goes off in your home, it goes off in the tank, too.

Temperature in all but the smallest tanks will be different in different parts of the tank. The water will be warmer at the top, since heat rises. To get an average temperature, put the thermometer *bulb* midway between the surface and the bottom.

Algae, tiny green plants, are always present in the water. When they are there in the right amount, you can barely see them. When algae grow too much, however, you can see them everywhere—on the inside of the tank, on rocks, gravel, and ornaments. Although some fish eat algae, there is sometimes just too much for even the biggest eater. Algae aren't really bad for the tank, but they can make it look messy. Too much heat and/or too much light makes algae grow.

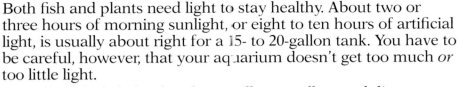

LIGHT

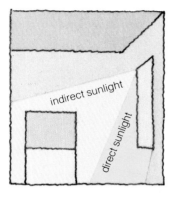
indirect sunlight

direct sunlight

Both fish and plants need light to stay healthy. About two or three hours of morning sunlight, or eight to ten hours of artificial light, is usually about right for a 15- to 20-gallon tank. You have to be careful, however, that your aquarium doesn't get too much *or* too little light.

With too little light, the plants will turn yellow and die, upsetting the balance of the tank. With too much light, algae will grow too quickly. Too much sunlight also makes the water too warm, especially during the summer months. And if the summer mid-day sun shines into the tank for a few hours, and then the tank is in the shade for a few hours, the fish may get sick from the change in temperature. It is best to keep your tank where there is sunlight, but not direct sun.

If sunlight is not available or convenient, you can use artificial light. There are many types of lights made to fit tanks. You can even use a regular lamp.

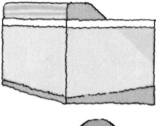

things to know about lighting

Light should come from above the tank so that it shines on the water in the most natural way. Some people light tanks from the back—but the tanks certainly don't look natural.

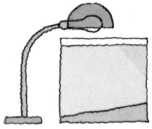

If artificial lighting equipment is used, it will come with a bulb, or tell you what size to get. Don't use a bigger bulb than suggested or it might overheat the water.

If you see streams of bubbles rising from your plants, it means that they are getting too much light and producing too much oxygen. Cut down on the amount of light until there are just a few bubbles.

There is no way to tell exactly how much light a particular tank will need. It takes trial, error, and a lot of patience. And, every time you add fish or plants to the aquarium, or take some out, the amount of light should be checked. You may need more or less.

Sudden changes in light are very upsetting to fish. If the room and the tank have been dark, don't suddenly turn on bright lights, even if you want to show your fish to a friend. Put on a small light across the room from the fish, and then wait a while before turning on brighter and closer lights.

FURNISHINGS

Fish are beautiful...but a tank with just fish, water, and a lot of electrical equipment isn't too interesting. Fish could live with nothing else—just as people could live in a house without furniture. But plants, gravel, rocks, and other decorations can make your tank more attractive and a better and more natural place for fish to live.

Fish show their own colors best in an old, established tank that has natural surroundings. In a new tank, with few furnishings, they will look paler in color.

plants

Plants are needed in a tank for many reasons besides just looking good. And different types of plants do different things for the tank and the fish. The plants shown here have different purposes. There are, of course, many other plants that can be used in an aquarium. The most important thing is to get plants that serve all the purposes discussed here. In return for all that the plants do for fish, the fish provide the kind of air plants need—full of carbon dioxide—and their wastes become fertilizer for plant roots.

Do not collect plants for your tank from streams or brooks, and don't use field or house plants. Buy your plants from a pet or aquarium store so that you can be sure they are clean and have no tiny (or large) bugs that might cause trouble. Replace your plants as they grow old or yellow, or get raggedy.

Amazon swordplant
(Echinodorus paniculatus)
can have either broad or
narrow leaves. It grows
slowly and seldom needs
thinning out.

*Plants are natural water
filters. During the day,
when there is sunlight,
plants take in the carbon
dioxide that the fish
breathe out, and give off
oxygen. At night, however,
in the dark, the plants
breathe out carbon dioxide
and breathe in oxygen. Although plants do let off oxygen during the day, they
don't really add much to
the water.*

Tape or eelgrass
(Vallisneria spiralis)
has leaves that grow up
to 18 inches long and
½ inch wide. They look best
planted near the rear of a
tank to form a back-
ground. They like bright
light and should be
thinned out once in a while.

*Small fish use plants as
food. The fish will nibble at
them until the leaves look
like lace.*

Duckweed *(Lemna)* is a floating plant that provides natural shade to the tank. Although it grows to cover the surface completely, it doesn't seem to stop oxygen from moving from the surface into the water. It may be difficult to grow in a tank with a complete hood and artificial lights. Lemna needs thinning so that it doesn't cover the surface too thickly.

Shade plants use up the sunlight, food, and oxygen needed by algae. When there are enough shade plants, the algae cannot develop, so the water stays cleaner.

Water milfoil *(Myriophyllum)* likes cold water best, but will also grow well in temperatures suitable for tropical fish. It has fine, feathery leaves that sway as the fish swim near them.

Egg-laying fish often leave their eggs on plants, especially plants with feathery leaves.

Pygmy chain swordplant *(Echinodorus tenellus)* grows to be about 2 inches high. It spreads out on runners and is a good bottom-growing plant.

Plant roots use and spread fish and plant wastes. Shy fish need plants to hide behind; active fish need plants to play around.

27

gravel and sand

Water plants grow well when their roots are tucked into gravel or sand. Also, gravel and sand make a more natural bottom than glass. You will need enough gravel to make a layer about 1½ inches deep. Build the gravel up higher in the back of the tank and slope it toward the front—just the way there is a slope to a river bottom. When the gravel is sloped, wastes and leftover food will drift to the front of the tank where they can be removed more easily.

Sand can be used instead of gravel. It should be of quartz or silica and should be bought at a pet store. Do not use seashore or sandbox sand—both contain too much lime (the mineral, not the fruit) and will hurt the fish.

Marbles, colored pebbles, and lead weights can also be used to hold plants in the water. Lead is the only metal that should be used in the tank, since it cannot rust. Shells should not be put in the tank, as they dissolve easily and add things to the water that might harm the fish.

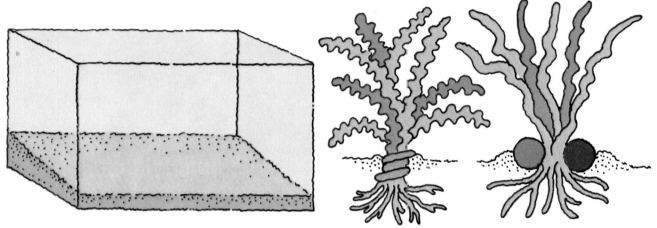

no soap

Your fish and even your plants can easily get sick. Additions to the tank can be harmful. Be very careful about what you put into the tank—including your hands if they are very dirty or if there is any soap on them. Never use soap on any part of your tank, its equipment, or furnishings. The smallest bit of soap can kill your fish. Wash everything in clean water with a clean brush before putting it into the tank. Especially with your first few tanks, buy all equipment and furnishings in a pet store. To be safe, wash even things that are marked "prewashed." And, when in doubt, leave it out.

rocks and other ornaments

Rocks not only look good in an aquarium, they also provide good hiding and resting places for fish. One or two large rocks are better than many small ones. Wastes and uneaten food can gather under small rocks, rot, and dirty the water. A large rock can be cleaned with less trouble.

Some rocks are too soft for use in aquaria; others have too much metal or lime in them. Unless you know a lot about rocks, buy them in a pet store. Choose rocks that do not have sharp edges that might hurt the fish. Red shale looks particularly nice. Instead of one or more of the rocks, you can use petrified wood.

Of course, you can also buy fake rocks and decorations made of concrete, like those make-believe castles and deep-sea divers. Some people like them...but they are very unnatural-looking and they usually collect wastes.

GETTING IT TOGETHER

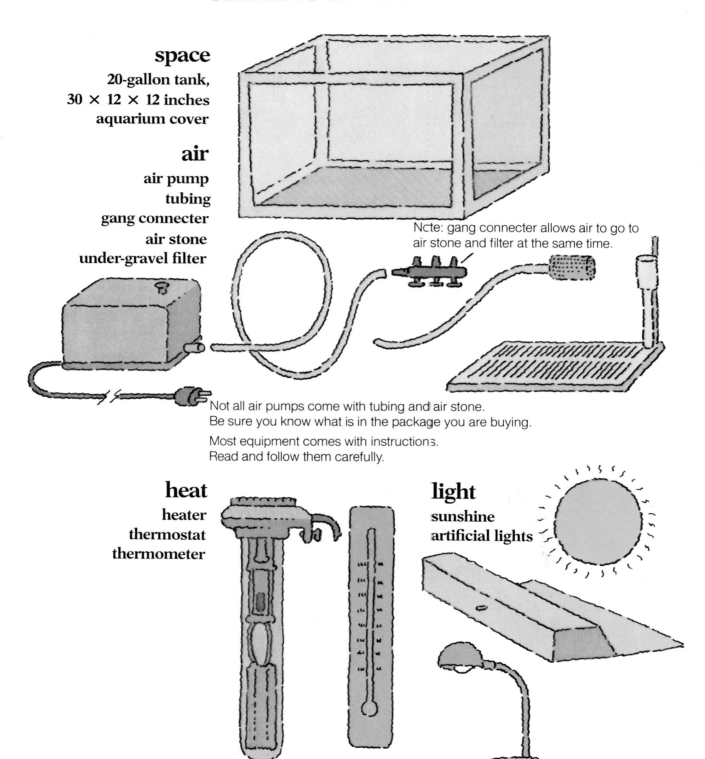

space
20-gallon tank,
30 × 12 × 12 inches
aquarium cover

air
air pump
tubing
gang connecter
air stone
under-gravel filter

Note: gang connecter allows air to go to
air stone and filter at the same time.

Not all air pumps come with tubing and air stone.
Be sure you know what is in the package you are buying.

Most equipment comes with instructions.
Read and follow them carefully.

heat
heater
thermostat
thermometer

light
sunshine
artificial lights

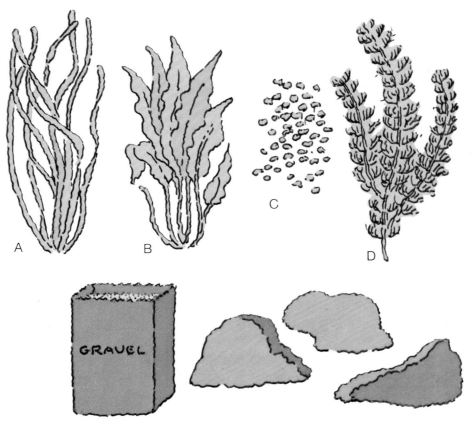

furnishings

plants

Eelgrass A
(Vallisneria spiralis)
**10 plants each about
10 inches tall**

Amazon swordplant B
(Echinodorus paniculatus)
2 plants

Duckweed C
(Lemna) just a little

Water milfoil D
(Myriophyllum) 2 plants
gravel
rocks

tools

plastic watering can
paper
large, shallow plastic pan
plastic scrubber
electrical outlet
kitchen or workroom sink
water
rags or sponges

Note: be sure can has sprinkler head so that plenty of air gets into the water.

PUTTING IT TOGETHER

1 Visit pet stores, a public aquarium, and friends with aquaria to see their tanks and to get ideas for your own.

2 Decide where you want to put your tank. Consider sunlight, location of electrical outlets, and the size of the tank. A 20-gallon tank weighs a lot when it is filled with water. You will need a table strong enough and large enough to hold it. The tank measures 30 x 12 x 12 inches.

Getting the tank ready for fish will take about a week.

3 Purchase all necessary equipment except fish. Reread earlier sections on the parts and needs of the aquarium as you go along.

4 Working at a sink, wash gravel in a shallow plastic pan. Do *not* use soap. Put gravel in pan, add water to cover it, and stir the gravel around. Pour off water. Repeat until water is clear when you stir the gravel. Don't try to hurry the job—it's dull, boring, and necessary. Badly washed gravel can kill your fish.

5 Scrub the tank and aquarium cover with plastic scrubber and plain water. Again, no soap. Make sure the tank and cover are absolutely clean, inside and outside, top and bottom. Rinse out completely.

6 Sorry, but now wash the gravel again. Now that it has had a chance to dry and settle, you will find that you did leave some dirt in it. Scrub rocks and any other ornaments you plan to add to the tank.

7 If you are using an under-gravel filter, wash it carefully and set it into the tank.

Some fish can tell the difference between colors. They know red, orange, and yellow from green, blue, and purple. Some fish have learned to tell the danger of a white net, and fishermen have had to dye their nets green or brown—more natural underwater colors.

33

8 Put the tank on a stand in its permanent place. Once you start adding things to the tank, especially water, it will be too heavy to move. Put gravel in the tank. The gravel should be about two inches deep at the back and slope to one inch at the front. Add rocks and other ornaments.

To work out the weight of a full aquarium, multiply the number of gallons the tank holds by 8⅓. A filled 20-gallon tank weighs about 167 pounds (76 kilograms).

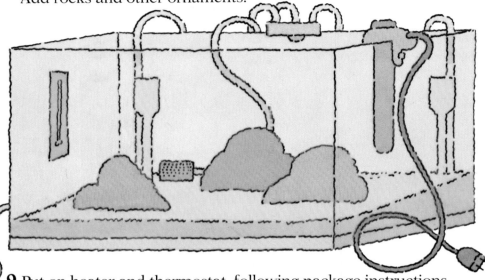

9 Put on heater and thermostat, following package instructions carefully. Do not plug in. If you have a separate heater and thermostat, connect them to each other, but do not plug in. Put the thermometer at the opposite end of the tank from the heater so that they do not interfere with each other.

10 If you are using an outside or bottom filter, put it in place, but do not plug it in.

11 Connect, but do not plug in, the air pump, tubing, and air stone.

Electricity and water are a dangerous combination. Make sure all electrical work is done carefully and correctly. Ask a parent or a friend who *really* knows about it to check your work.

A boy bought two fish, but when he got home he had three. How can this be?

He had two flounders —and one smelt.

12 Place a clean sheet of paper over the gravel and ornaments so that they are not disturbed when you put the water in. Using the watering can, so that the water gets plenty of air in it, fill the tank half full of cool, but not cold, water. Remove paper.

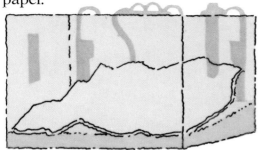 

13 Rinse off plants and remove any yellow or dead leaves. Push plants into the gravel up to their crowns—the place where the leaves start to grow. Heap gravel around the roots. Extra gravel, marbles, or lead weights may be needed to make the plants stand up straight. Use the taller plants at the back of the tank, shorter ones near the front and around the rocks. Do not add floating plants yet.

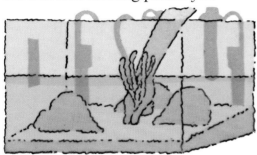 

A Eelgrass
B Amazon swordplant
D Water milfoil
  Duckweed
  (Not shown; floats on top)

14 Using the watering can, add water until the tank is filled up to 2 inches from the top. Pour very carefully so that you don't disturb the plants and stir up the gravel. Don't pour all the water in the same place.

15 Have someone recheck your electrical systems. Plug in the heater, filter, and air pump and turn them on.

16 Add floating plants.

The fish come later

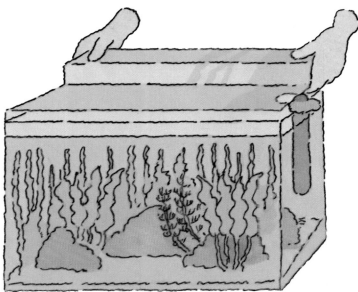

17 Put on cover and lights. Plug in lights. If you are only using artificial lights, leave them on for eight to ten hours a day. If there is some sunlight, reduce the amount of time the artificial lights are on. One hour of indirect sunlight is equal to about four hours of artificial light.

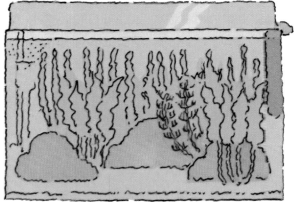

18 Leave the tank without fish for one week to give the water time to age and yourself time to be sure everything is in working order. Make sure, for example, that the tank does not leak—some of them do even when brand-new. Check the temperature each day to be sure that the thermostat and heater are working correctly. Remove and replace any plants that die. If all or most of one type of plant dies, try another variety that has the same look and use. Notice if streams of bubbles are coming from the plants or if algae are growing too quickly—if so, there is too much light. See if the plants are turning yellow from too little light. Make necessary adjustments.

19 Read about fish and decide exactly which ones you want. Make up a list of the fish and decide which ones to buy first. You should not plan to buy all your fish at the beginning. It is better for the fish, and more interesting for you, to start with just a few fish and add more as you go along.

20 Buy your starter fish. A good group to begin with might include

- a pair of hatchetfish or pearl danios to swim at the surface
- a pair of kissing gourami, rosy barbs, or platies, and a small school (four or five) of tetras for the middle level
- a single angelfish to swim wherever it chooses
- a bronze catfish to live at the bottom of the tank and clean up wastes and algae.

This selection makes a good balance of personality, color, and location for a starting tank. If you want other kinds of fish, just be sure to choose ones that will fit into the community. You should not, for example, decide to leave out the hatchetfish and have barbs, platies, and gourami. You would have the right number of fish, but they would all be swimming in the middle level and the surface of the tank would be empty.

21 Bring the fish home. Fish are often packed in plastic carrying bags. By the time you get them home, the water in the bags is usually a different temperature than the water in your tank. If you pour the fish directly into your tank, the change in water temperature, along with the discomfort of traveling, may harm your fish. Float the traveling bag, still closed, in the aquarium. Within an hour, the water in the bag will get to be the same temperature as the water in the aquarium. Open the bag and let the fish swim out. Don't try to hurry them.

22 It will take the fish several hours to get used to their new home and companions. Feeding them will only confuse and possibly upset them. Wait about twelve hours before you feed your fish and then just feed them a little.

Do not overfeed the fish.

23 Add more fish to your tank as your fish get accustomed to each other—and as your allowance allows. Choose them carefully to fit into the community. The most fish you should ever have in a 20-gallon tank is forty

---

Which fish is most well-known?   ·   *A starfish*

In the natural state, of course, fish don't get seasick. But they can get carsick when they travel in small containers for long distances. If you have to move your aquarium far away, don't feed your fish for about a week before the move.

FOOD

Don't overfeed your fish. More fish get sick from overfeeding than from any other mistakes.

Feed your fish once a day, at the same time each day, and a very little bit each time. They should not be given more than they can eat in ten minutes. At first, measure out a pinch of food and give them part of it. Wait until they finish it, and if ten minutes is not up, give them more. In about a week you will work out how big a pinch they can eat in ten minutes. Then you can give it to them all at once. In warmer weather, increase the amount of food a *little*, and feed twice a day.

Fish can go without food for up to a week. If you miss a feeding, do not try to make up for it by giving them extra food. When you plan to be away for a week, you don't have to find someone to feed your fish. You can, little by little, lower the temperature of the tank about 5° during the week before you leave. Fish need less food in colder temperatures. And they will, of course, be getting some food by nibbling at the plants.

If you are going away for longer than a week, do ask a friend to feed your fish. To make it easy on your friend and your fish, wrap up packets of food with the right amount for each feeding in them. Write on the packet when you want it given to the fish. Even if your friend knows all about fish, she or he doesn't know *your* fish. A few weeks of wrong feeding can upset the tank and make the fish sick.

Try some variety in fish food. You'd get tired of eating even your favorite food at every meal. Stick to one main food and give a different food at least once a week.

You can train some of your fish to come to you at feeding time. Tap gently, once or twice, on the side of the tank just before feeding. After a few weeks, if you feed at the same time each day, the fish that can learn to come will be waiting for you. It's fun—but don't overfeed and confuse your fish by showing the trick to friends when it isn't feeding time. And don't tap on the tank unless you are going to feed the fish.

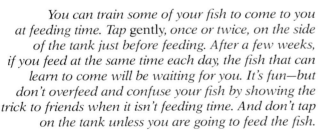

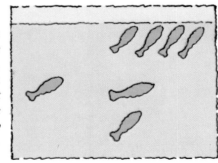

A healthy fish *always* looks hungry. Don't let anyone tell you to feed your fish because they "look hungry."

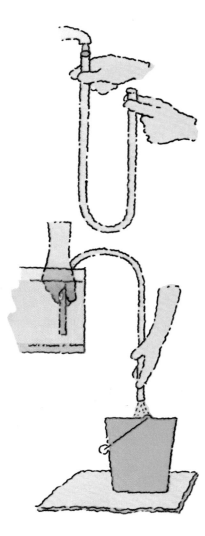

HOUSEKEEPING TOOLS
siphon

A siphon is used to get water out of the tank and to remove sediment (waste material) that has collected in the gravel. You usually have to siphon at least once a month to keep the tank really clean.

   To siphon you need a clear piece of plastic tube about 4 feet long and ¾ inch in diameter. Most pet stores sell siphons. Put a pail on some newspaper on the floor near the aquarium. Get some rags and sponges ready since some water *always* spills. Pinch one end of the tube closed with one hand. Hold the other end of the tube under the faucet and slowly fill it with water. When the tube is almost full, pinch the faucet end shut, too. Keeping both ends shut, put one end into the aquarium and the other into the pail. Open your fingers, but don't let go of the tube. The water will go from the aquarium into the pail. If you are siphoning off waste material, keep the aquarium end of the tube aimed at whatever you want to get out of the tank. Watch out for small fish. Any water that is removed while siphoning off wastes must be replaced. Use water that has been aged for twenty-four hours and pour it from a watering can so that there is plenty of air in it.

dip tube

A dip tube is easier to use for small clean-up jobs than a siphon. You can buy one at most pet stores. The dip tube is a glass tube about ½ inch in diameter and 1 foot long with a bulb at the bottom. To use it, cover the top of the tube with your index finger and then put the other end into the water over the waste materials. Now take your finger off the top. The wastes, along with some water, will go into the tube. Then, before you take the tube from the water, put your finger back over the opening. Take the tube out of the water—the wastes and water really will stay in—hold it over a bowl, and lift your finger off the top. The wastes and water will go into the bowl.

scraper

Sometimes algae build up on the sides of the tank and need scraping off. You can buy a scraper at a pet store or you can make your own from a *single*-edged razor blade. You can also use steel wool that has no soap in it.

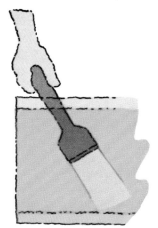

bottle for aging water

A bottle of water—a gallon, if possible—should be kept aging for emergency use. Wash the bottle without soap, make sure it is really clean, and let it air for a day before putting water in it.

small extra tank

An extra tank is very handy for use as an infirmary for sick fish, an isolation area for new fish, or a holding zone while you are changing water. A 5-gallon tank is just about the right size. You can also use a large glass bowl with a wide top and high sides. Use a dinner plate for a cover. Put lead washers or small corks at four places around the top of the bowl to keep the plate from sitting right on top and shutting out the air.

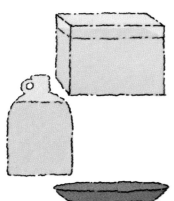

net

A rectangular fish net is best because it has the largest mouth. You may need several nets of different sizes to pick up different-sized fish. A tiny fish could get hurt in a big net—and so could a fast-moving big fish in a small net. Use a net big enough to make a bag that can be closed with your free hand once the fish is in the net. Or use two smaller nets of the same size. Never touch a fish with your hand. You might disturb the protective film on its skin. Never use a strainer made of metal or hard plastic, which could hurt the fish. You have to be patient to net fish, because they often get scared and dart away. Take your time. Relax. And get help if necessary. When you have netted the fish, put it into water again as soon as possible.

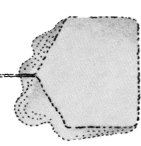

notebook and pencil

Make notes about your aquarium and what happens in it. They're fun to read later on, and will help you to find and correct mistakes. Write down when you get each fish, what its habits are, and how the new fish has changed the habits of other fish in the tank.

Get a magnifying glass. Things seem different when you really look at them.

water problems and solutions

1 Cloudy water Water gets cloudy because the fish are getting too much food and some of it is rotting. To clear it up, don't feed the fish for a few days while the cloud settles to the bottom. Then, if any scum is left floating on top of the water, you can blot it up with a paper towel. Lay a towel on top of the water let it get wet, and then peel it up carefully from one end. Repeat with fresh pieces of paper until the scum is gone. Use a dip tube or siphon to remove waste materials from the bottom. When you feed the fish again, give them less food than before. If the cloud keeps coming back, you may need another scavenger fish or a few more bottom plants.

2 Green water Green water is caused by algae. This won't hurt the fish, but it's hard to see your pets when the water and the sides of the tank are green. Use a scraper on the sides of the tank and a siphon or dip tube to pick up the glop that falls to the bottom. If the water is very green, you may have to siphon some off and replace it with aged water of the right temperature. To stop the algae from coming back, cut down on the amount of sunlight and/or add some floating plants.

3 Dead water Water sometimes gets too cloudy, or too green, or has too much carbon dioxide in it. Then the fish have to stay at the surface, opening and closing their mouths to breathe. The water has little or no oxygen in it and needs changing. Siphon off some water and replace it with aged water until you can change the entire tank. Make sure there are no dead plants or fish in the tank. Remove algae and wastes and check all equipment and tank furnishings. Be sure your tank is not overcrowded and that you are not overfeeding.

What is the difference between the earth and the sea?

One is dirty and the other is tide-y.

cleaning the tank

If you have no filter or air pump, you should siphon off wastes and replace about 10 percent of the water each week in order to keep the tank and water clean. If you do have a filter and pump, change about 10 percent of the water once a month, or when there is an emergency. Keep a supply of aged water for replacement and emergency use. If you have no aged water, and the fish are at the surface gasping for air, gently splash the water to increase the amount of oxygen in the water. Then change the water as soon as possible. Changing more of the water than 10 percent will take two days because of the time needed to age the water.

changing the water

1 Put fresh water in a bowl or pan or extra aquarium to age for twenty-four hours. This water will be for fish storage while you are changing the aquarium water and cleaning the tank.

2 Unplug electrical equipment. Siphon off half of the water in the aquarium.

3 Using the dip net, scoop the fish out of the aquarium and into the aged water. Be patient about netting fish.

4 Usually you don't have to take more than half of the water out of the tank in order to clean the tank. If the water and the tank are very dirty, however, remove more now.

5 Clean the tank by scraping, scrubbing, and wiping. Use plastic scrubbers and no soap. Clean rocks and other furnishings.

6 Use a dip tube and siphon to get wastes off the bottom. Remove and replace any dead plants.

7 Plug in all electrical equipment. Make sure all equipment works and is clean.

8 Add water to tank.

9 Let water in tank age for twenty-four hours before returning fish to tank. Make sure that the water in the tank is the right temperature and that it is almost the same as the water in the storage tank. Fish should not be changed from one temperature to another and should never be put into water of a lower temperature.

Water evaporates. Watch the water level in your tank. When needed, add aged water of the right temperature. When you add water to a tank that has fish in it, be sure to use a plastic watering can. That way there will be plenty of air in the water, and the water won't fall with too much force.

A word about water

Water is different in different parts of the country. In some places it can be too acid or too alkaline. Both are alright for people and plants, but not too good for tropical fish. Sometimes a chemical has to be added to the water to make it right for fish. In most places the water just needs aging—sitting around for a day or so.

The pet store people will know about water conditions in your area and can tell you if anything has to be done to the water. You must remember to ask, however, since they might not think to mention it to you.

sick fish

Fish do get old, and hurt, and sick. As fish get older, they get sort of humped in the middle and their fins split and fray. They are not as active as usual. When fish get sick, their dorsal fins often sag instead of standing up straight. Fish with the most common illness, "ich" (ichthyophthirius), are covered with white spots.

A fish that is too old or badly hurt often cannot be saved. It should be removed from the tank so that it does not die unnoticed and foul the tank. If you have a bully in your tank that fights with other fish, and hurts them badly, you may have to give up the bully to save your other fish.

A sick fish can often be saved. Remove it gently from the tank and put it into a large bowl of aged water. Do not feed it. Make a list of all the things that make the fish look and act sick and take the list to a pet store for discussion. Some fish diseases can be cured with a simple medicine. Follow package directions carefully. Never return a fish to the tank until it has been completely well for a few days. A sick fish can infect a whole tank.

Healthy fish

Old fish

Sick fish

why fish get sick

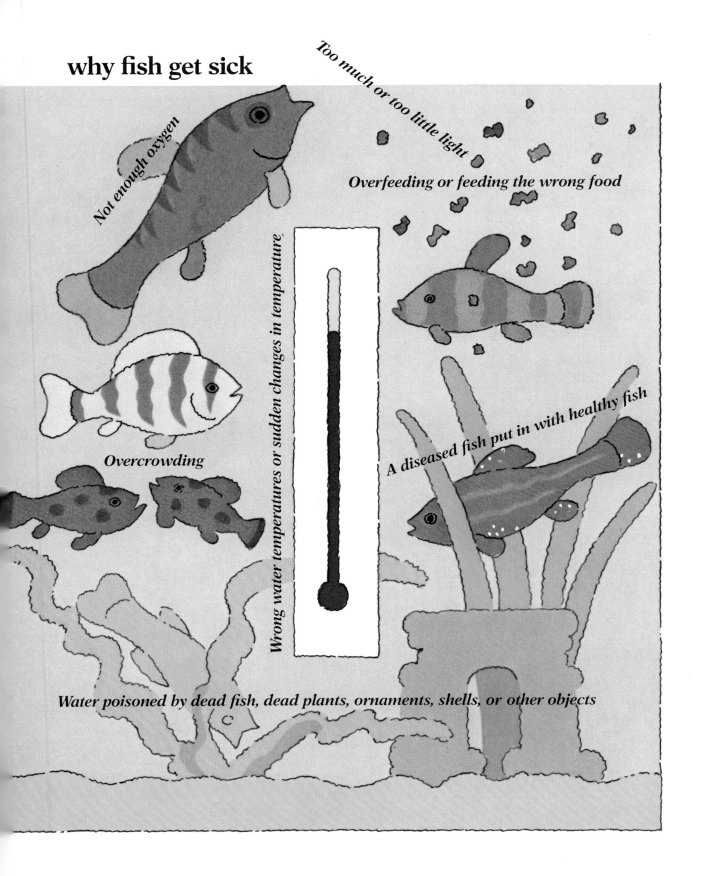

Not enough oxygen

Too much or too little light

Overfeeding or feeding the wrong food

Wrong water temperatures or sudden changes in temperature.

A diseased fish put in with healthy fish

Overcrowding

Water poisoned by dead fish, dead plants, ornaments, shells, or other objects

fishy but fact...

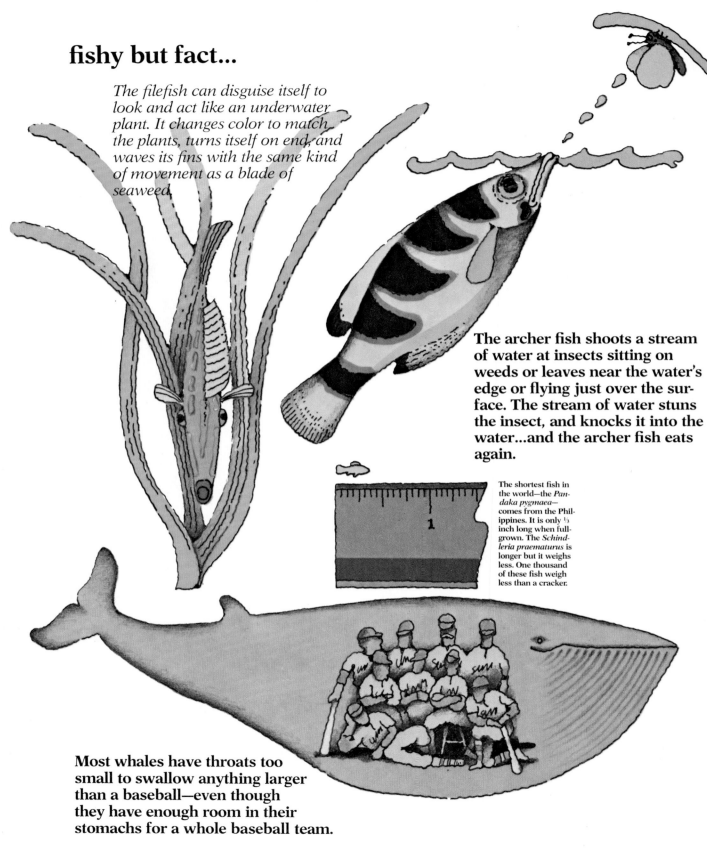

The filefish can disguise itself to look and act like an underwater plant. It changes color to match the plants, turns itself on end, and waves its fins with the same kind of movement as a blade of seaweed.

The archer fish shoots a stream of water at insects sitting on weeds or leaves near the water's edge or flying just over the surface. The stream of water stuns the insect, and knocks it into the water...and the archer fish eats again.

The shortest fish in the world—the *Pandaka pygmaea*—comes from the Philippines. It is only ⅓ inch long when full-grown. The *Schindleria praematurus* is longer but it weighs less. One thousand of these fish weigh less than a cracker.

Most whales have throats too small to swallow anything larger than a baseball—even though they have enough room in their stomachs for a whole baseball team.

The sleeper (dormitator) looks as if it would make a fine aquarium fish. It is a bright blue and yellow on its sides, and emerald and brown on its back and fins. Like the goldfish, it could be kept at room temperature with no need for heating equipment. But sleepers cannot be kept as pets. When taken into captivity, they faint—especially the males. Even if the sleepers can be gotten to a tank, they will continue to faint if the tank is moved or the water disturbed. Sometimes they even die of fear, or maybe it's anger—no one has ever asked them.

The oolachan is a species of fish from the northern Pacific. The body of the fish is so full of fats and oils that it is often used as a candle. The Alaskan Indians dry the fish and then pull wicks of rush or bark through them.

The ocean sunfish produces more eggs than any other fish—up to 300 million at a time, each measuring .05 inches in diameter. The ocean sunfish is only ⅛ of an inch long when it hatches. At that time it is almost round, with five spikes around its body. As it grows it changes shape almost completely. Sometimes the spikes turn into needles. At other times the fish becomes taller than it is long. As an adult, it may be 11 feet long and weigh a ton. It has a tiny mouth and is harmless to people, but unfortunately it has a fin like a shark's and is all too often killed out of fear and ignorance.

The mormyrid fish has a trunk like an elephant. The trunk is used for feeding in the murky bottoms of lakes and rivers.

What part of a fish is like the end of a book?  **The fin is.**

1 3 5 7 9 11 13 15 17 19 PD/P 20 18 16 14 12 10 8 6 4 2
1 3 5 7 9 11 13 15 17 19 PD/C 20 18 16 14 12 10 8 6 4 2
Library of Congress Cataloging in Publication Data

Sarnoff, Jane.
    A great aquarium book.

    SUMMARY: A beginner's guide to creating a basic
aquarium, with information on selecting fish and
providing for them a comfortable, healthy environment.
    1. Aquariums—Juvenile literature.   [1. Aquariums.
2. Tropical fish]   I. Ruffins, Reynold.   II. Title.
SF457.S25   639'.34   75-39298